MAKE IT
OUT ALIVE
IN THE
OCEAN

Claudia Martin

PowerKiDS press™
New York

Published in 2018 by The Rosen Publishing Group
29 East 21st Street, New York, NY 10010

Produced for Rosen by Calcium
Editors: Sarah Eason and Jennifer Sanderson
Designer: Emma DeBanks
Picture Research: Rachel Blount
Illustrator: Venetia Dean

Picture credits: Cover: Shutterstock: 3DMI (br), Ase (bg). Inside: Shutterstock: Akedesign 9,
Andrey Popov 42, Anekoho 21, Anton_Ivanov 15, Jeffrey B. Banke 25t, Denis
Churin 39, Alessandro De Maddalena 30, De Visu 37, Designua 36, Laura Dinraths
18, Feathercollector 7, 12, Focal point 5tr, Holbox 10, 47, Juhana Lampinen 26, Garuna Liu 34,
Mangax 5b, Mycteria 23, Nejron Photo 32, Off Axis Production 22–23, Ottmaasikas 33, PHB.cz/
Richard Semik 20, Martin Prochazkacz 31, Sayhmog 38, Serg64 41, Sheykhan 5c, Beth Swanson
19, Think4photop 8, Jellis Vaes 4, VanHart 6, Vlad61 13, Vibrant Image Studio 44, Wims-eye-d
23, David Wingate 11, Sara Winter 16, Yellow Cat 40bl, Andrey Yurlov 14, Zurijeta 28; Wikimedia
Commons: Katerha (www.flickr.com/photos/katerha) 27.

Cataloging-in-Publication Data
Names: Martin, Claudia.
Title: Make it out alive in the ocean / Claudia Martin.
Description: New York : PowerKids Press, 2018. | Series: Makerspace survival | Includes index.
Identifiers: ISBN 9781499434767 (pbk.) | ISBN 9781499434705 (library bound) |
ISBN 9781499434583 (6 pack)
Subjects: LCSH: Survival at sea--Juvenile literature. | Wilderness survival--Juvenile literature.
Classification: LCC G525.M35 2018 | DDC 910.4'52--dc23

Manufactured in China.

CPSIA Compliance Information: Batch BS17PK: For Further Information contact Rosen
Publishing, New York, New York at 1-800-237-9932

Please note that the publisher **does not**
suggest readers carry out any practical
application of the Can You Make It?
activities and any other survival
activities in this book.

A note about measurements:
Measurements are given in U.S.
form with metric in parentheses.
The metric conversion is rounded to
make it easier to measure.

CONTENTS

CHAPTER 1
SURVIVE
THE OCEANS

You are about to be set adrift in a boat in the middle of a vast ocean. Completely alone, you must find your way to land. If that is not enough of a challenge, here are the rules: You cannot take any food, drink, shelter, or matches. How will you survive?

Will You Make It Out Alive?

You will be left in an **inflatable** boat with two oars. You will have a life jacket and a pocketknife. You can dress in your choice of clothing and footwear. Apart from these essentials, you must provide yourself with food, water, and shelter by making your own tools and equipment. You are allowed to use anything that floats past your boat, whether it is a recyclable man-made object or a natural material. You will also be provided with a backpack. In this, you will find some interesting materials and tools.

You will be set adrift in a boat just 8 feet (2.5 m) long.

What Is in Your Backpack?

The following materials and tools are in your backpack. When you come across a "Can You Make It?" activity in this book, you must choose from these items to construct it. Each item can be used only once. Study the list carefully before you set off. You can find the correct solutions for all the activities on page 45 of this book.

Nylon string

Can You Make It?

Materials
- 11 extra-long garden stakes
- Bowl
- Coin-size piece of cork
- Electrical tape
- Large plastic bottle
- Large tarp
- Magnet
- Marker
- Metal sewing needle
- Nylon string
- Plastic cup
- Plastic twist ties
- Red plastic garbage bag
- Slim wooden dowel, 3 feet (1 m) long
- Slim wooden dowel, 2 feet (0.5 m) long

Tools
- Pair of scissors

Pair of scissors

Survival Tip
Use the Internet to look up all the items in your backpack before you begin your journey. Make sure that you understand what they are and how you might be able to use them.

Magnet

WORLD
OF OCEANS

Before you are cut loose in your boat, take a moment to find out about the world's oceans and the dangers you will be facing. The oceans cover 140 million square miles (360 million sq km). This is more than 70 percent of Earth's surface.

World of Oceans

There are five oceans. From largest to smallest, they are: the Pacific, Atlantic, Indian, Southern, and Arctic. Seas are areas of an ocean that are partly enclosed by land. For example, the Caribbean Sea is part of the Atlantic Ocean and is partly enclosed by the Caribbean islands and the coast of the Americas. Over millions of years, the water in the oceans and seas has become salty. When rain falls over land, it soaks through soil and rocks, **dissolving** small amounts of the **mineral salts** that make up the rocks. Rivers wash this salt into the oceans.

Key
1 Atlantic Ocean
2 Pacific Ocean
3 Indian Ocean
4 Southern Ocean
5 Arctic Ocean

The largest ocean, the Pacific, covers about one-third of Earth's surface. The smallest, the Arctic Ocean, is always partly covered by ice.

Never Still

The oceans' water is constantly in motion. Currents are great "rivers" of water that flow from one region of the ocean to another. Some currents are caused by wind blowing across the ocean surface. Other currents are caused by differences in the temperature and saltiness of the water. Cold and salty water sinks, so warmer water rushes in to take its place. Near the equator, the sea is warmed by the sun to an average of 80° F (27° C) at its surface. At the poles, where the sun's rays are weaker, the sea surface is only around 28° F (-2° C). This temperature difference creates global movements of water.

Wind blowing across the surface of the ocean causes waves. The stronger the wind and the wider the ocean it has blown across, the higher the waves. Occasionally, a combination of currents and storms can create waves more than 100 feet (30 m) high. These monsters are called rogue waves.

Antarctic icefish live in water so cold that some of them have a special antifreeze in their blood to keep it from freezing.

OCEAN
PEOPLES

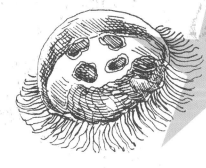

Waves and storms make the oceans a hazardous place. However, some traditional peoples, such as the Moken of the Andaman Sea in Asia, spend most of their lives at sea. They can teach us how to survive at sea using only handmade tools.

Life Afloat

Traditional Moken spend nine months of every year at sea, living in wooden sailing boats called *kabangs*. *Kabangs* are shaped from a single tree trunk. First, the trunk is hollowed out. It is then heated over a fire until the wood is soft, so that it can be shaped and widened. The **prow** and **stern** are carved into a forked shape, like an open mouth. This shape makes the boat stable and also creates a foothold for the Moken when they climb aboard after a dive. **Flotillas** of *kabangs* sail together, following the winds and fish. During the rainy season, when storms make the ocean dangerous, the Moken move ashore. They build huts on stilts at the water's edge.

A traditional kabang's *sail and shelter are made from stitched-together leaves from pandanus trees. The shelter is for sleeping and cooking.*

Diving for Fish

Moken dive underwater to catch fish. They are armed with a throwing spear made from a bamboo stem with a sharpened tip. They catch only the fish they intend to eat. The Moken are skilled **free divers**, holding their breath as they hunt as deep as 100 feet (30 m).

The Moken also build underwater "islands" to attract fish. **Coral reefs** teem with fish, but many reefs are too deep underwater to reach. Instead, the Moken dangle a rope in the water above a reef, attached to a float made of hollow bamboo stems. A bundle of palm leaves is tied to the rope about 30 feet (9 m) below the surface. Tiny **organisms** grow on the leaves, attracting reef fish to feed on them. The Moken dive to their "islands" to spear the fish.

FIERCE FACT!
The Moken can see underwater twice as clearly as other people because they are so practiced at diving for fish, shellfish, and sea cucumbers.

Today, most Moken have moved ashore. Their way of life is under threat from **overfishing** and tourism.

OCEAN
SURVIVOR

Steve Callahan was sailing alone in the middle of the Atlantic Ocean when his yacht was smashed during a storm. Steve grabbed some supplies and climbed aboard his inflatable life raft, which became his home for the next 76 days.

Using His Supplies

Steve's supplies included a pocketknife, spear gun, pencils, plastic sheeting, and three solar **stills**. Solar stills use the sun's heat to make freshwater from seawater. Steve had to make many modifications to his stills before he could get them to work. He also used his plastic sheeting to collect rainwater. He scooped up sargassum seaweed and ate the crabs, shrimp, and fish he found on it. He set traps to catch seabirds, using empty containers and fish guts as bait.

Barnacles and weed started to grow on the bottom of Steve's raft. These attracted a school of mahimahi fish, which he speared. Any fish that he could not eat immediately, he hung up to dry in the sun, so that it was preserved. Disaster struck when a speared mahimahi tore a hole in his raft. He patched the leak with a scrap of nylon, held in place with a twisted fork.

Mahimahi can grow to more than 4 feet (1 m) long.

Drifting with the Current

A sextant is a tool that can measure the angle between a known star, such as Polaris (the North Star), and the horizon. Knowing this angle lets you calculate your distance north or south of the equator. Steve made a sextant with his pencils. His calculations revealed that the current was carrying him toward the Caribbean.

Eventually, Steve spotted an island and paddled toward it. As he was wrapping himself in plastic sheets to protect himself while crashing ashore in the surf, Steve heard a shout. It was from a boat of fishermen, who had noticed the seabirds swimming around the raft, attracted by Steve's school of mahimahi.

FIERCE FACT!
Steve Callahan had drifted 1,800 miles (2,900 km), from the mid-Atlantic to the island of Marie-Galante, part of Guadeloupe in the Caribbean Sea.

An inflatable life raft has a cover to protect its occupants from waves and sun. It does not have an engine.

CHAPTER 2
WATER ALL AROUND

Your challenge has begun! You are alone in your inflatable boat, surrounded by ocean water as far as the eye can see. You must meet your most urgent survival need: finding water that is safe to drink.

Too Salty

Even though you are surrounded by water, you should not drink it. On average, seawater is 3.5 percent salt. That means that every cup of seawater contains more than a teaspoon of salt. Although a little salt in your diet does you no harm, drinking seawater is not good for you. If you drank a cup of seawater, you might feel less thirsty for a moment, but you would soon start to feel sick. That is because your body needs to get rid of all that excess salt.

Seabirds, such as the albatross, must get rid of the salt they swallow in seawater and fish. They pass it out through a salt gland on their beak.

FIERCE FACT!
Earth's saltiest body of water is Don Juan Pond, in Antarctica, which is 40 percent salt. It is not an ocean but a small, shallow lake.

The Red Sea is the saltiest region of ocean water. It contains more than 4 percent salt.

Dehydration

It is your kidneys' job to get rid of salt and other waste products by expelling them from your body in your urine, or pee. However, to wash out all the extra salt, your kidneys will need extra freshwater. Your body is about 60 percent water, and it needs a constant supply of freshwater to keep it working properly. To do their vital job, your salt-threatened kidneys will turn to your body tissues to supply the freshwater they need.

If you continue drinking seawater, your kidneys will keep taking water from your body until it contains so little water that it will not be able to function. This is called dehydration, which can be deadly if it is not treated. Signs of dehydration include severe thirst, exhaustion, dizziness, and confusion.

COLLECT RAINWATER

Rain and snow do not contain salt, so if you can think of a way to collect the water that falls from the sky, you will be able to drink it. Think about whether any of the materials you have in your boat could be used to collect water.

Evaporation

As the sun heats the ocean, water **evaporates** from the surface. As it evaporates, the seawater leaves behind all its salt. The water, now a **vapor**, mixes with the air. The warm, moist air rises into the sky. As it rises, the air cools. Cool air cannot hold as much moisture as warm air, so the water vapor **condenses**, or turns back into a liquid. This is how clouds form: They are floating masses of water droplets. When the water droplets in a cloud get too heavy, they fall as rain, or snow if it is very cold.

Water is constantly on the move: It evaporates from the ocean, condenses in clouds, then falls as rain.

Make a Container

Do not wait for it to start raining before you create a container to collect water. Examine the contents of your backpack to see if there is anything that will help you. Perhaps you are wearing some waterproof clothing. The fabric's waterproof covering keeps it from **absorbing** water, so the water pools on the surface instead. Using string or cord, you could construct a water-collection pool and funnel, so that you can drink directly from a plastic poncho or tarp.

If you are in the Arctic or Southern Ocean, you could break off a chunk of iceberg and suck on it.

Collecting Freshwater

In polar regions, icebergs are another source of freshwater. Tall icebergs form on land from **compacted** snow before floating into the ocean. In contrast, sea ice, which forms on the surface of the polar oceans, is frozen seawater and not safe to drink.

FIERCE FACT!
Fish eyes and spine bones contain water that is almost free of salt. Catch a large fish, then suck on the eyes and break apart the spine.

PURIFY SEAWATER

On the previous pages, you examined how the sun's heat makes freshwater out of seawater. You can perform the same process by making your own solar still. A solar still copies the way nature makes rain.

Solar Still

The principle of a solar still is that it uses the sun's heat to cause evaporation in a container of seawater. For this reason, the still must be transparent, or see-through, to allow the sun's rays to shine through. When the seawater evaporates, it becomes pure water vapor, leaving behind its salt. The water vapor rises, so the still must be enclosed to prevent the vapor from escaping. If the water vapor touches a plastic or glass surface, it cools and condenses, forming water droplets. Finally, a still needs a collection chamber to hold the water drops that trickle downward.

FIERCE FACT!
In sunny weather, a still 1 foot (30 cm) wide and 1 foot (30 cm) deep would provide around 1 cup of drinking water in a day.

At this huge salt flat in Bolivia, South America, all the water evaporated from an ancient lake, leaving behind a crust of salt.

Make a Solar Still

From the supplies in your backpack, you will need to make:

→ A container to hold seawater
→ A transparent cover on which water vapor will condense into liquid water
→ A means of collecting the water.

Can You Make It?

Step 1
Think about which item from your backpack could be a container for seawater.

Step 2
Which item could be used as a cover for your still? It will have to fit over the top of your container, so you may need to make modifications to its shape.

Step 3
How will condensed water be collected in your still?

Step 4
Pour water from your collection chamber directly into your mouth, or empty the seawater container and use it to drink.

Cover and collection chamber

Container for seawater

Condensed water

Seawater

CHAPTER 3
GO FISHING

Now that you have a supply of drinking water, apply your maker skills to filling your empty stomach. The oceans are filled with food, from fish to **invertebrates**, such as squid and crabs. How will you catch your food?

Life-Saving Seaweed

Seaweeds are plantlike organisms called **algae** that drift in the ocean. Many seaweed **species** are eaten around the world, such as the nori seaweed that is used to wrap Japanese sushi. Not all seaweeds are **edible**, but some, such as sargassum, are nutritious. Sargassum is chewy and has a bitter flavor, but it is a source of protein and energy. Sargassum is also home to crabs, shrimp, and other small creatures, so it is a like a natural fishing line.

If it is collected from the open ocean rather than a beach, all parts of sargassum are edible. This includes the gas-filled spheres that keep it afloat.

Fish Food

Freshwater fish cannot be eaten raw, but many fish that live in saltwater are reasonably safe to eat without cooking if you are in a life-and-death situation. This is because the salt kills off many of the **bacteria** that could make you unwell. However, do not eat fish that looks sick, with a nasty smell, sunken eyes, or loose flesh. You must also avoid poisonous fish and any with **venomous** spines. It is not always easy to spot a poisonous fish, although many of them have bony plates, bristles, or rough scales. Poisonous fish are often found in shallow waters around coral reefs or **lagoons**.

In hot weather, uneaten fish can spoil within hours. To preserve fish, cut it into thin strips, and hang it in the sun to dry by threading it on a string or pole. If the flesh smells bad, do not eat it. If you start to vomit, you will quickly dehydrate.

FIERCE FACT!
Every year, more than 120 million tons (109 million tonnes) of fish are caught for eating. The world's most popular food fish is herring.

When threatened, this poisonous porcupine fish inflates its body. This makes it harder for an attacker to swallow.

CAST
YOUR NET

A fishing net is a mesh made of knotted fibers. Nets are thrown into the sea, suspended in water using floats, or dragged behind a boat. If you catch fish in your net that you do not need to eat, make sure you release them unharmed.

Finding Fibers

The earliest fishing nets were made from plant fibers, such as grasses or thin strips pulled from the bark or roots of trees. Modern nets are made from extra-strong man-made fibers such as nylon. Seaweed alone is not strong enough to be woven. However, some makers have experimented with combining seaweed with tough fibers from trees, such as eucalyptus, weaving a fabric that is natural, **durable**, and comfortable. Consider whether you have any materials in your backpack that could be used to knot a net.

A fishing net is made of cords knotted in a diamond pattern.

Knotting a Net

To make a net, you must knot together strings in a check or diamond pattern. There are many methods, so if you cannot master this one, it does not matter as long as your end result holds together. Cut 10 equal pieces of string or cord. Lay them side by side. First, join strings 1 and 2 together by knotting them around each other. In the same way, knot together string 3 with string 4, string 5 with 6, 7 with 8, and 9 with 10. This is your first row of netting.

Large fishing nets can tangle endangered animals, such as dolphins and sea turtles. Be aware of how your net could impact the environment.

An Alternating Pattern

For the second row, leave out strings 1 and 10. Knot together string 2 with 3, string 4 with 5, 6 with 7, and 8 with 9. For the next row, return to the pattern of the first row, knotting together string 1 with 2 and so on. Adjust the space between your rows depending on the size of fish you want to catch.

FISHING ROD

If you use a fishing rod rather than a net, you will catch only enough fish to meet your immediate needs. This is kinder to all the sea creatures that will escape being unnecessarily tangled in a net.

Back to Basics

In a life-and-death situation, all you truly need for a fishing rod is a line, a hook, and bait. For your line, look through your backpack to see if there are any materials you could use. Other options could be your shoelaces, tough seaweed stems, or even a thread unraveled from your clothing. Bear in mind that these strings will not have the strength of a store-bought fishing line. If you do feel a pull on your hook, do not rely on hauling in the fish using your line. Instead, scoop up your catch using a container, spare clothing, or even your bare hands.

The hook needs to be tied securely to the line. It is for holding bait and should catch in a fish's mouth if the bait is taken. If you saw an old soda can floating by, the pull tab would be ideal for this job. You could also try a bent hairpin or paper clip, or a sharpened piece of wood or plastic.

Fish like to swim in shady, sheltered water, so they may cluster in the shadow of your boat.

The Bait

Bait is used to attract fish to take a bite. If you have some unwanted, old food, such as fish guts, it would be ideal bait. Insects, if you can catch them, would also work. The Moken use floating palm islands to attract tiny organisms and, later, fish. You could attempt a similar approach by using seaweed. Finally, try anything that catches a fish's eye, such as seabird feathers, strips of your clothing, jewelry, or bright pieces of plastic.

FIERCE FACT!
Scientists believe that fish that live in sunlit surface waters can spot different colors. Deep-sea fish probably see only light and dark.

Bright feathers could attract fish.

CHAPTER 4
SIGNAL FOR HELP

Lost and alone at sea, a good survival strategy would be to attract the attention of a passing boat or airplane. Do not waste your energy by shouting or waving, unless rescue is very nearby. Think about using bright colors and light.

Shipping Lanes

Shipping lanes crisscross the oceans. Large vessels, such as cargo ships and cruise liners, use the shipping lanes. The routes are determined by the quickest voyage between one port and another, and by currents and prevailing winds. In a particular area, the wind usually blows from one direction. This is the prevailing wind.

Ships do not have to use shipping lanes, but they often do, making them the busiest parts of the ocean. If you see ships passing in the distance, paddle toward them to increase your chance of being spotted. However, cargo ships often have small crews, so there may not be a lookout to see you. Also, beware of being caught in the **wake** of these powerful ships.

A passing cargo ship could rescue you from your ordeal, but only if its crew spot your signals.

MSC AMSTERDAM

Use Light

Use a mirror or other reflective surface, such as a belt buckle, to shine the sun's rays into the eyes of a passing airplane pilot or ship's lookout. Flash the light on and off. This signal can be seen for several miles.

If you have a magnifying glass or glasses lenses, you could start a raft fire. Flames will be highly visible at night, and the smoke could be seen during the day. Collect driftwood or floating packing crates, then dry them in the sun for several days. Build a wooden raft, heaped with **flammable** materials, then tie it to your boat with a long rope. Collect scraps of dry clothing or wood shavings. Using your lens, concentrate the sun's rays on your scraps until they catch on fire. Transfer the burning scraps to your raft, and prod it to a safe distance away.

FIERCE FACT!

The longest ship ever built was an oil tanker. *Seawise Giant* was 1,504 feet (458 m) long. Standing on end, it would be longer than some of the world's tallest buildings.

DISTRESS FLARES

Flares are often used to signal for rescue, both on sea and land. They create a brilliant light that can be seen for many miles. Flares can be held in the hand or shot into the sky with a pistol-like flare gun.

Ancient Makers

The Chinese army used the earliest known flares in the thirteenth century. Small rockets were shot into the sky using gunpowder. The flares were timed to explode in midair, sending a signal to friendly troops. Today, red-colored flares are commonly found in ocean survival kits. Flares get their light from a **chemical reaction** made by combining a fuel, such as sawdust, charcoal, or aluminum, with an explosive substance, such as potassium perchlorate.

Red flares are international distress signals.

Rocket Science

You will not be able to build a flare on your boat, but with the help of an adult, you can experiment with the principle of rockets when you get home.

The power for your rocket will come from a chemical reaction between vinegar and baking soda. When these are mixed, they create the gas carbon dioxide, which you will see as bubbles. In a sealed space, these bubbles will build up the pressure. That force can shoot a small rocket into the air.

Put on safety goggles. In a large, open space, away from people, animals, windows, and anything that can break, combine a little vinegar and baking soda in a bottle. Press a very soft **projectile** lightly into the top of the bottle. Quickly put the bottle on the ground, and step backward. You could experiment with different quantities of vinegar and baking soda to see what sends your projectile highest.

VOLUMES

150

When mixed together, baking soda and vinegar create bubbles of carbon dioxide.

RESCUE KITE

Flying a balloon or kite above your raft could attract the attention of rescuers. Make one out of shiny, fluorescent, or bright-colored material. Your balloon or kite must be strong enough to withstand the ocean winds.

Diamond Kite

Lift is the force that sends a kite into the air. Unlike a balloon, a kite is heavier than air. Gravity would make it fall to the ground, but lift carries it into the sky if its "sail" catches the wind. The wind cannot pass through the surface of the kite. It must flow around it. As the wind does so, the air flowing underneath the kite puts more pressure on the kite than the air flowing above it. This pushes the kite into the sky. If the wind stops, the kite will fall. Kites are lightweight, so they can be lifted by gentle winds.

A symmetrical, diamond-shaped kite is aerodynamic.

The shape of a kite is important. It needs to be **symmetrical**. A diamond shape is **aerodynamic** because it lets the kite cut through the air smoothly. In contrast, a rectangular kite would collide with the air and corkscrew. A kite's strings should also be attached symmetrically for balance.

Make a Diamond Kite

From the supplies in your backpack, you will need to make:

→ A strong, but light, frame for your kite
→ A bright-colored sail
→ A string to tether your kite.

Can You Make It?

Step 1
Think about which items in your backpack could form a frame for your kite. How will you tie them together?

Step 2
Which item could you cut to make a sail? What will you use to stick it to the frame?

Step 3
Which item will you use as a string? Consider how it can be tied securely to the frame. How can you tie it so that the frame is symmetrical?

Step 4
You could complete your kite by attaching a tail of streamers.

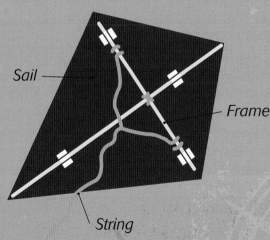

Sail

Frame

String

CHAPTER 5
STAY SAFE

To survive your challenge, you must keep your boat and your body in good condition. Check your boat and yourself for signs of damage or sickness, and keep clean. Dealing with waste is particularly difficult if the waters are shark-infested.

Boat Care

Keeping waste on board your boat will breed bacteria, which could make you sick. Do not leave food scraps on board. When you need the toilet, go over the side, or use a container that you do not need for storing drinking water, then pour the waste over the side promptly. Be aware that throwing waste overboard could attract sharks. However, peeing while you are in the water will also attract them. You are safer if you stay on board. Wash down the boat every day. If it rains, take the opportunity to wash your skin, as it will be caked in salt from dried seawater. Over time, the salt will make your skin sore.

Be careful not to puncture your boat with your shoes, pocketknife, or other sharp equipment. Check frequently for any signs that it is deflating. If it is, locate the hole quickly so you can patch it. Steve Callahan used a scrap of nylon and a bent fork to repair his boat. Consider which items you could use from your backpack.

Sharks do not always swim with their tall dorsal fin above the water. In fact, most like to attack prey from below.

Shark Attacks

Sharks are not known to deliberately attack boats, but they may attack you if you are in the water. Do not go for a swim if you are bleeding from a cut or wearing shiny jewelry, since this will attract them. If you see a shark approaching, climb back on board as quickly as you can. If you are attacked, fight back fiercely. Think about how you could make a sharp tool to prod an aggressive shark in the eyes, where they are most vulnerable.

Great white sharks live in all oceans, apart from in colder waters around the poles.

FIERCE FACT!

Only three species of sharks attack humans regularly: great white, tiger, and bull sharks. More than 70 shark attacks are reported every year.

WILD WEATHER

Watch out for the signs of an approaching storm: darkening clouds, thunder and lightning, and increased wave height. If you are hit by a storm, your priorities are to stop your boat from **capsizing** and to keep warm and dry.

Capsize!

If the waves grow into steep, white-capped peaks, you risk being overturned if they strike the side of your boat. Using your paddles, steer the boat so the prow is hitting the waves first. By presenting a smaller surface to the waves, your boat has less chance of being rolled. Cover your boat with waterproof sheeting or a tarp, to keep yourself and your supplies dry. If water does slosh aboard, bail it out using a container or bag, so that you do not sink.

Every year, 2,000 seafarers are lost at sea.

After the Storm

Once the storm has died down, dry off the deck using an absorbent cloth. It is important to dry your shoes and clothes as quickly as possible to prevent bacteria breeding in the damp cloth. You will also get cold if you spend a long time in wet clothes. Getting extremely cold could lead to hypothermia, when the body's temperature drops below 95° F (35° C). Symptoms include severe shivering, confusion, and, if left untreated, the shutting down of the body's systems.

Take off wet T-shirts and pants, and hang them to dry on a pole or string. Leave on wool clothes if you do not have a change of clothing. A useful property of wool fibers is that they can absorb a large quantity of water, then release it into the air, still keeping you fairly warm inside. Keep on your waterproof outer clothes, and add extra layers, plus a hat, to keep in your body heat. Stuffing bird feathers inside your clothing will add **insulation**. Keep out of the wind, which will increase your heat loss.

FIERCE FACT!
Wind speed is measured using the Beaufort Scale, from 0 to 12. Storms are rated 10 or above, with wave heights more than 29 feet (9 m).

> *Seals are kept warm, or insulated, by a thick layer of fat called blubber.*

GET UNDER COVER

Adrift in the open ocean, you have no protection from the sun, wind, and rain. Enlist your maker skills in erecting a sun canopy, which will also double as a rain shelter and a warm place to sleep.

Sun Exposure

One of the greatest dangers faced by **castaways** is the sun. Wear sunglasses and a hat, and keep your skin covered to prevent eye damage and sunburn. When the sun's rays shine down on the water, they reflect off it. If you do not have sunglasses, give your eyes protection from the water's glare by tying a bandanna or cloth loosely over your nose. Getting too hot could lead to sunstroke, which is when your body is unable to cool itself, causing your temperature to soar dangerously high.

Sun Canopy

When constructing your sun canopy, consider your basic problem: On the rolling waves, how will you make your structure stable? If you were on land, you could drive stakes into the ground, but you cannot puncture your boat. Experiment to see which shapes are self-supporting. Whatever the shape of your structure, it should have both upright and horizontal posts firmly lashed to each other.

This fishing raft in Taiwan has a wooden shelter.

Make a Sun Canopy

From the supplies in your backpack, you will need to make:

→ A stable, self-supporting frame for your canopy
→ A waterproof, **opaque** cover for the frame.

Can You Make It?

Step 1
Think about which items in your backpack could make a stable frame for your canopy.

Step 2
Which items could tie your frame together securely?

Step 3
Which item could be laid over your frame as a waterproof sunshade?

Step 4
Consider how you could make your structure more sturdy to keep it from toppling over in high seas. Hint: Cuboid structures that are lower to the ground are sturdier than taller cuboid shapes. Triangular shapes are also sturdy.

Waterproof sunshade

Frame

Ties

CHAPTER 6
RESCUE!

There are two ways you could survive this challenge: if rescuers spot you, or if you reach land. You have an important decision to make. Should you try to navigate toward land, stay where you are, or allow yourself to drift?

Drift with the Current?

Steve Callahan allowed himself to drift on the South Equatorial Current, which carried him westward from the mid-Atlantic Ocean to the Caribbean. Should you let yourself drift? In each ocean, surface currents tend to move in great circles, called gyres, with separate gyres operating on either side of the equator. In the northern hemisphere, the gyres turn clockwise. In the southern hemisphere, they turn counterclockwise.

> An understanding of ocean currents could save your life.

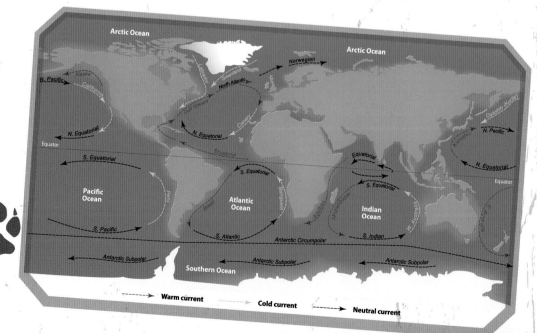

Sail with the Wind?

The easterly trade winds also helped Steve Callahan on his westward journey. Easterly winds blow from the east to the west. Trade winds are the prevailing winds in the **tropics**, between 30° **latitude** north of the equator and 30° south. Wind is air moving from one area to another, caused by the sun's uneven heating of Earth. Warm air rises, so cooler air flows in to fill its place. At the equator, the hot air rises. Cooler air blows in from the north and south. Earth's turning makes this air move westward. For this reason, north of the equator, the trade winds blow from the northeast. South of the equator, the trade winds blow from the southeast. Outside the tropics, the prevailing winds are usually westerlies.

If you think the prevailing winds could boost your chances of survival, consider how to make a sail using items in your backpack, such as tarp, sticks (perhaps several bound together to make a strong mast), and rope.

FIERCE FACT!
Salvadoran fisherman José Salvador Alvarenga holds the record for surviving the longest time adrift at sea. He spent 13 months on the Pacific Ocean.

Modern sails are constructed from extra-strong man-made materials, such as carbon fibers.

ANCHORS AWEIGH

If you are in a shipping lane or under a busy air-traffic route, you may decide that your best option is to remain where you are and await rescue. How do you keep yourself from drifting?

Sea Anchor

An ordinary anchor is a heavy device, usually made of metal and tied to a cable or chain. It connects a ship with the seabed to keep it from drifting. However, far out at sea, the water is too deep for an ordinary anchor. The weight of the length of cable or chain required might sink the ship. Instead, a sea anchor is used. Sea anchors cannot stop movement entirely, but they can slow the speed at which a ship drifts with the wind and current.

A metal anchor will keep a ship from moving when its curved "fluke" catches on the seafloor.

The principle of a sea anchor is that it is dragged in the water behind the ship to slow its movement. To do so, it needs to present a large surface area to the flow of water. Store-bought sea anchors are often made of cloth and shaped like a parachute or cone. The wider end faces into the current's flow, so the cone fills with water.

This simple store-bought sea anchor is cone-shaped.

Make Your Own Anchor

To construct your own sea anchor, improvise with the items in your backpack. A tarp or spare clothing tied to ropes would form a basic anchor. Experiment to see if weighing down your anchor slows your movement or speeds it up. A more sophisticated anchor could make use of a wooden or metal frame. Sea anchors work best when used just below the water's surface, so think about your materials carefully.

FIND NORTH

Knowing which way is north will help you determine what direction to take or whether to let yourself drift on the currents. Pinpointing north will also keep you from wasting energy paddling in circles.

Use a Watch

For this method of finding north, you need a watch with hands set to the actual time, not **daylight saving time**. You must also know whether you are in the northern hemisphere or southern hemisphere. This method does not work if you are in the tropics.

In the northern hemisphere, point the watch's hour hand at the sun. Now draw an imaginary line from the center of the watch dial, midway between the twelve o'clock mark and the hour hand. Take the shortest distance between the hour hand and 12, so if the hour hand is on two o'clock, draw your line at one o'clock, midway between 12 and 2. This imaginary line is pointing south. In the southern hemisphere, reverse the method. Point the twelve o'clock mark to the sun. North is halfway between 12 and the hour hand.

In the northern hemisphere, point your watch's hour hand at the sun. In this example, south is at one o'clock

South

North

40

Digital Method

Another method, which can be performed with a digital watch, requires you to note the times of sunrise and sunset. Note the times in 24-hour style: So 7:00 p.m. is 19:00. Subtract the time of sunrise from the time of sunset, then divide that number by two. Add the result to the time of sunrise. In the northern hemisphere, this is the time when the sun will be due south. In the southern hemisphere, it is when the sun is due north.

If the sun sets at 8:00 p.m. (20:00) and rises again at 7:00 a.m., subtract 7 from 20. That gives you 13. Dividing by 2 gives you 6 ½. Add 6 ½ hours to the time of sunrise, which was 7:00 a.m. So in the northern hemisphere, the sun will be directly to the south at 1:30 p.m (13:30).

If you have a digital watch set to the correct time, note the times of sunrise and sunset. Remember that the sun hardly ever rises or sets directly to the east or west.

USE A COMPASS

The easiest way to find north is by using a magnetic compass. A compass needle always points to magnetic north. It is possible to make your own compass using a few basic items.

Homemade Compass

At the center of Earth is an iron core. Iron is magnetic, making Earth a giant magnet. A magnet has a center of force, called a pole, at each end. A magnetic field runs between the poles. When you put pieces of magnetized metal in a magnetic field, they line themselves up with it. This is what a metal compass needle does in Earth's magnetic field, making it point toward magnetic north. A compass needle needs to be able to spin freely. It also needs to be magnetized. This can be done by stroking it with a magnet around 50 times in the same direction.

The needle of a magnetic compass always points to north.

Make a Compass

From the supplies in your backpack, you will need to make:

→ A magnetized compass needle
→ A water-filled container
→ A holder for the needle, so that it will float on the water.

Can You Make It?

Step 1

Think about which items in your backpack could be used to create a magnetized compass needle. How would you magnetize the sewing needle?

Step 2

Which item from your backpack could hold seawater?

Step 3

Which **buoyant** item could the magnetized needle be pressed into, so that it floats freely on the water?

Step 4

Your needle will swing to point north–south. Use one of the methods on the previous pages to determine which end is north. Choose an item from your backpack to draw an "N" on the needle-holder. Write an "N" for north using the marker.

Magnetized needle

Buoyant item

Seawater container

SIGNS OF LAND

During daylight hours, keep watch for signs of land. At night, listen for the sounds of human activity or increasing noise from seabirds that may be roosting on land. Smells, such as those of gasoline or vegetation, may be carried on the wind.

You Survived!

One sunny afternoon, you spot a large cloud on the horizon that is not moving. Other clouds drift past, but this cloud remains still. You suspect that the cloud has formed over an island. You grab your paddles and row toward it. You notice many seabirds flying to and fro, in greater numbers than over the open ocean. Is that growing dark smudge really an island? At last, you see a flotilla of Moken *kabangs* and shout as loud as you can. The Moken offer to throw you a rope so they can tow you to the island. Your ordeal is over!

Clouds tend to form over islands as moist air blows in from the sea. The air rises over the sun-warmed island and condenses into clouds.

ANSWERS—
DID YOU MAKE IT?

Were your makerspace survival skills up to the test? Did you select the best equipment for each "Make It Out Alive" activity? Check your choices against the answers below.

Page 17 Solar Still
Large plastic bottle • Plastic cup
Pair of scissors
Use the plastic cup to collect seawater. You could cut the base off the plastic bottle, then fold the bottom upward to form a collection chamber. Place the bottle securely over the cup. Drink directly from the collection chamber.

Page 29 Diamond Kite
Electrical tape • Nylon string
Red plastic garbage bag
Wooden dowel, 3 feet (1 m) long
Wooden dowel, 2 feet (0.5 m) long
Pair of scissors
To make the frame, tie the two dowels together using string, with the longer dowel placed vertically. Cut a diamond from the garbage bag, and stick it to the frame with electrical tape. Tie the string to both sides of your diamond kite, so that it is symmetrical.

Page 35 Sun Canopy
11 extra-long garden stakes
Large tarp • Plastic twist ties
To make the frame, build a cuboid out of garden stakes. Secure the frame with twist ties. Use the tarp as a cover. For a more stable canopy, use a wide base for your cuboid and make it low to the ground. Alternatively, your canopy could have a tripod-shaped frame with added horizontal supports.

Page 43 Compass
Bowl • Coin-size piece of cork
Magnet • Marker
Metal sewing needle
The sewing needle can be used as the compass needle. Stroke the needle with the magnet 50 times, always stroking in the same direction. Use the bowl to collect water. Press the needle through the middle of the buoyant cork. Write an "N" for north using the marker. Fill the bowl with water, and add your cork compass needle.

GLOSSARY

absorbing Soaking up or drawing in.

aerodynamic Having a shape that cuts smoothly through air.

algae Plantlike living things often found in water.

bacteria Tiny living things that can cause disease.

barnacles Shelled sea creatures that attach themselves to surfaces.

buoyant Able to float.

capsizing Overturning in the water.

castaways People who are stranded in a place where there are no other people, usually because of a shipwreck.

chemical reaction When two or more substances combine to form new substances, often giving off heat.

compacted Pressed firmly together.

condenses Changes from a gas into a liquid.

coral reefs Mounds or ridges formed of living coral and coral skeletons.

daylight saving time The practice of putting clocks forward between spring and fall, so that sunset occurs later in the evening.

dissolving Mixing with a liquid and becoming part of it.

durable Hard-wearing.

edible Safe to eat.

evaporates Turns from a liquid into a vapor or gas.

fibers Thin threads of animal, plant, or man-made material.

flammable Easy to set on fire

flotillas Groups of boats.

free divers People who dive underwater holding their breath.

inflatable Capable of being filled with air.

insulation A material or substance that prevents heat from going out of, or into, something.

invertebrates Animals without a backbone, including insects and shellfish.

lagoons Shallow stretches of water separated from the sea by an island or reef.

latitude Measure of the distance north or south of the equator.

mineral salts Crystals that form naturally, including sodium (salt).

opaque Impossible to see through.

organisms Living things.

overfishing Catching so many fish that not enough remain.

projectile An object that is thrown forward.

prow Pointed front end of a boat or ship.

shipping lanes Routes regularly used by ocean traffic.

species A group of similar living things that can breed with each other.

stern The back of a boat or ship, which is often blunt, not pointed.

stills Devices that use evaporation and condensation for separating liquid mixtures.

symmetrical Having parts that match, or reflect, each other.

tropics A region around the equator.

vapor Gas from a substance.

venomous Able to inject a poisonous substance.

wake Trail of disturbed water behind a boat or ship.

FURTHER READING

Books

Bell, Samantha. *How to Survive Being Lost at Sea* (Survival Guides). North Mankato, MN: The Child's World, 2015.

Rake, Jody S. *Endangered Oceans: Investigating Oceans in Crisis* (Endangered Earth). North Mankato, MN: Capstone Press, 2015.

Spilsbury, Louise. *Surviving the Sea* (Sole Survivor). New York, NY: Gareth Stevens, 2016.

Westerfield, Mike. *Make: Rockets*. San Francisco, CA: Maker Media, Inc., 2014.

Websites

Due to the changing nature of Internet links, PowerKids Press has developed an online list of websites related to the subject of this book. This site is updated regularly. Please use this link to access the list: www.powerkidslinks.com/ms/ocean

INDEX